# Options Trading For

# Beginners

*The Beginner's Guide For Investing And Generating A Consistent Cash Flow Without Effort With Options And Swing Trading*

## Byron McGrady

# Table of Contents

Introduction ............................................................................................8

CHAPTER 1  Rolling Positions ...............................................................10

How to Roll a Covered Call? ............................................................ 11

How to Roll the Short Strangle? ...................................................... 13

How to Roll a Short Call Spread? .................................................... 15

CHAPTER 2  Trading Varying Time Frames .........................................16

Weekly Options Trading .................................................................. 16

Advantages of Weekly Options ................................................... 17

Disadvantages of Weekly Options .............................................. 18

Buying Weekly ............................................................................. 18

Selling Weekly ............................................................................. 19

Spreads ........................................................................................ 20

Intraday Trades ............................................................................... 20

Intraday Trading Challenges ....................................................... 20

Protective Put .............................................................................. 22

Directional Options Trading ........................................................ 23

High Volatility Options Intraday Strategy .................................. 24

CHAPTER 3  Swing Trading With Options ...........................................26

What Is Swing Trading? ................................................................... 26

Swing Trading Options .................................................................... 28

Going Long on a Stock ................................................................. 29

Shorting Stock Using Put Options ............................................... 31

CHAPTER 4  Understanding Trading Orders .......................................34

Mechanism of Trading Orders ........................................................ 36

Different Types of Trading Orders ................................................................ 38

    Market Orders ................................................................................................ 38

    Limit Orders .................................................................................................... 38

    Stop Orders ..................................................................................................... 39

    Day Order ........................................................................................................ 39

Preparations for Placing an Order ................................................................ 40

Some Other Order Types ................................................................................ 41

**CHAPTER 5  Market Environment** ................................................................ **44**

Trends and Ranges ......................................................................................... 45

    Trends .............................................................................................................. 46

Trend vs. Range .............................................................................................. 46

    Countertrend Participation .......................................................................... 47

    Turning Points ................................................................................................ 50

**CHAPTER 6  Q&A to Help You Get the Most Out of Trading** ................... **54**

  1.   Why Is It Better to Trade in Options Than Other Forms of Investing? 54

  2.   What Are Some of the Ways That I Can Limit My Losses? ............... 54

  3.   What Are the Differences Between Puts and Calls? ......................... 55

  4.   What Assets Can I Trade-In? ............................................................... 56

  5.   What Are Some of the Characteristics of a Kind Options Trader? .... 56

  6.   Can I Trade-In Options Even if the Market Is Going Down? ............. 57

  7.   Is it Safe to Invest in Options? ........................................................... 58

**CHAPTER 7  Financial Freedom** ..................................................................... **60**

No Freedom ..................................................................................................... 60

Temporary Freedom ....................................................................................... 61

Permanent Freedom ....................................................................................... 62

Luxurious Freedom ......................................................................................... 63

**CHAPTER 8  Habits and Mindset of The Financially Free** ........................ **66**

Positive Thinking ............................................................... 66

Habits ................................................................................ 67

Self-discipline ................................................................... 68

Knowledge......................................................................... 69

Invest in Your Health......................................................... 70

Be Your Own Cheerleader................................................. 71

Be Goal-Oriented .............................................................. 72

Have a Plan........................................................................ 73

Be Accountable ................................................................. 74

Organization...................................................................... 74

**CHAPTER 9 Stocks Vs Options**.............................................**76**

**CHAPTER 10 Basics Of Options** ............................................**80**

Example of a Call Option.................................................... 80

Example of Put Option ...................................................... 81

**CHAPTER 11 The Time Value**.................................................**84**

**CHAPTER 12 Time Decay**......................................................**90**

**CHAPTER 13 Volatility Strategies** .........................................**94**

Historical Volatility............................................................ 96

Implied Volatility ............................................................... 97

**CHAPTER 14 Four Primary Greek Risk Measures**.................**100**

Theta ............................................................................... 101

Vega ................................................................................ 101

Delta................................................................................ 102

Gamma............................................................................ 103

Rho (p)............................................................................. 104

Minor Greeks .................................................................. 104

**Conclusion** .........................................................................**105**

# Introduction

If you have heard about the world of options trading, you might be wondering what investment you can make with options. You can make money out of trading options with anyone, whether you are a complete beginner or an experienced trader.

This guide will introduce you to Options Trading basics, and how it fits into the world of financial markets. We'll show you what options are, how they work, and how you can use them to your advantage

Options are very different from stocks since they're designed as derivatives. That means that options are tied to an underlying asset (stock, index, or commodity) and are traded outside of their relationship with that asset. They're considered more speculative than conservative investments. Stocks were designed as equity investments, which means that they represent ownership in the firms that issue them. Even though you can't cash out your shares before they mature, they provide a reliable way to earn passive income.

It is one of the most profitable and exciting ways to earn money. Although options trading can be complicated, it is not difficult to understand. In this article, we'll cover the basics, strategies, and information you need to know about options trading.

Options trading is similar to investing in stocks and bonds, except instead of buying shares of a company or buying paper for cash; you are buying an option on it.

Options trading is a type of derivative trade. It is the practice of buying and selling options contracts to control the price of stocks, commodities, indices, foreign currency, and other financial assets. Options are financial securities that give the holder the right to buy or sell a particular asset at a specific price and date.

Investors use options to speculate whether they believe that a stock's price will go up over time. If the investor anticipates that stock to increase, they will buy an option to gain exposure to that increase. If they do not predict that the price will increase, they may sell their option.

Remember this is not a complete guide on options trading. It is intended to give you a general idea of how options trading works. Before you begin trading options, it's important to know a little about what they are and how they work.

# CHAPTER 1

## Rolling Positions

Sometimes options traders wish to adjust positions they hold in the market. When this happens, it means the trader's market outlook has changed. It is possible to roll a short or long option position.

The term rolling refers to changing the outlook on the underlying security of an option. This change is often driven by a change in the outlook of the markets and positions held on certain trades. In such situations, a trader is often worried that certain positions will be assigned.

Rolling is like making a different turn other than the one initially planned. Think, for instance, you leave home heading to the grocery store only to end up at the movies. This is very similar to what rolling is about.

Rolling aims to either deter or cancel the assignment. Managing positions through rolling is an advanced technique that should only be applied by seasoned traders and experienced investors. Therefore, as an intermediate trader, you need to thoroughly understand this process before applying it.

Anytime that a trader rolls a position, they will be purchasing options very close to a current position in the marketing then sell this position to start another one. This process will cause small, minute, but significant tweaks to the trader's options' strike prices.

This will shift the expiration times further out, so positions do not expire as initially planned. Even then, this process is not a guarantee that the strategy will work. In extreme cases, rolling will only compound losses, so only experienced traders should apply this technique.

## How to Roll a Covered Call?

When you hold covered calls, you can choose to sell them to reduce the cost of holding them in long positions. When rolling calls forward, you will improve the break-even position and make it easier to succeed in the long run. However, you need to know if a position should be rolled on and when to do so. For instance, should rolling of a position occur twenty days to expiration or possibly at expiration?

Also, just about any trader can write a covered call. The most crucial thing is to manage such a position appropriately. Certain factors should be considered when rolling a position, especially near expiration Fridays.

First, you need to confirm whether the underlying stock is suitable for this kind of management. Then you will need to confirm the option chains for statistics involving the current and following month.

Now use the Ellman Calculator and enter the statistics to determine whether the dates are viable for rolling management. The first-month goal for initial returns stands at 2%–4%. With this information, you will finally need to conduct a thorough evaluation chart, technical information, and the prevailing market conditions. This way, you will comfortably be able to adjust your trades to benefit more.

If the stock price increases and you have no intention of selling the stock, you will need better management skills and high assignment risks simply because the covered call you have is now in-the-money. As such, you choose to purchase all your covered calls to cancel out any obligation to sell the stock. At this stage, it is advisable to then sell a call option that has little chance of being assigned at a better strike price.

The common strategy when a stock forecast or objective changes is to adopt a rolling process. Seasoned traders usually adapt rolling covered calls. Even then, as a trader, you should understand that there is no specific formula for the implementation of a rolling plan. For instance, as a trader, you may be wondering the current covered call should be shut down and replaced with yet another call that is in line with the new changes.

## How to Roll the Short Strangle?

Rolling is the process of adjusting options strategies that a trader sets up. There are varied reasons why traders adjust their trades. These include erroneous initial predictions, changing market positions, and news that will affect a stock's performance.

Now on a strangle strategy, you always have a negative delta on the put and a positive delta on the call option. Therefore, we can deduce that we have a neutral delta in this instance. A neutral delta is okay at the onset. However, if the position remains that way, then you lose money. As a trader, you desire to make money; therefore, you want this movement to be huge when there is movement in the stock price. As such, you may use gamma, which will ensure the price goes up. However, should the stock price remain constant without any movement, then you will lose money.

The short strangle is sometimes considered by traders as a very risky strategy. However, as an experienced trader who knows what they are doing, this is not necessarily the case. Here is a look at some circumstances where risk is reduced by rolling action.

First, the premium is considered rather rich. As it is, a short straddle requires a trader to sell a put option and a call option based on an underlying option with similar expiration dates and strike prices. The best ones offer a very rich premium under near-the-money or at-the-money conditions.

Also, short straddles must have expiration dates that are within one month or less. It is time decay that causes the value of options to decline. Therefore, short straddles should be limited to only short-term options. Time decay often happens extremely fast within the first month.

Traders should focus their eyes on the current price and the strike price then note the relationship. It is advisable to close positions once it becomes practically possible. This should happen, especially when positions begin to move in-the-money. It is always a great idea to close at a profit because time decay will affect the trade value.

## How to Roll a Short Call Spread?

When you roll a spread, the action is like rolling a single option. A trader who rolls a short call spread is most probably exit a position in a timely fashion with the strike prices moving down or up. The difference between rolling the short call spread and an individual option is that you will be engaged in a four-way trade with the short call spread. You will essentially be trading four different options instead of the usual two. This means opening two new positions while closing two existing ones.

If you implement a rolling process on a stock option position, be careful not to compound your losses because this is quite possible. Therefore, if you are confident about your initial predictions, you should try and stick to your game plan. Alternatively, you could choose to exit the strategy rather than roll and incur even larger losses.

This roll management process applies to most two-legged trades and not just the short spreads. Rolling also applies to other formations, including back spreads and straddles.

# CHAPTER 2

## Trading Varying Time Frames

### Weekly Options Trading

Weekly options are listings that provide an opportunity for short-term trading as well as plenty of hedging possibilities. As the name states, they have an expiration time of exactly one week; in general, they are listed on Thursday and expire the following Friday. While they have been around for decades, they have primarily been the domain of investors who work with cash indices. This exclusivity level changed in 2011 when the Chicago Board of Options expanded the number of ways they could be traded, especially to make them more easily acceptable to traders like you. Since then, the number of stocks that can be traded weekly has grown from 28 to nearly 1,000.

In addition to having a short time frame, weekly options differ from traditional options in that they are only available three weeks out of the month. They are also never listed in the monthly expiration style. The week that monthly options expire, they are technically the same as weekly options.

## Advantages of Weekly Options

The biggest benefit of buying into weekly options is that you are free to purchase exactly what you need for the exact trade you are looking to make without worrying about coming up with extra capital or dealing with more options than you currently need. This means if you are looking to start a swing trade, or even an intraday trade, weekly options will have you covered. For those looking to sell, weekly options provide the ability to do so more frequently, rather than wait a month between sales.

Weekly options trades are also useful in that they lead to reduced costs for trades that have longer spreads, such as diagonal spreads or calendar spreads, as they can sell weekly options against them. They are also useful to higher volume trades as they are useful for hedging larger positions and portfolios against potential risky events. When the weekly options bind the market, the market can still be utilized through the iron butterfly or iron condor.

## Disadvantages of Weekly Options

The biggest disadvantage when it comes to weekly options is the fact that you will not ever have very much time for a trade to turn around if you make the wrong choice in the first place. If you are selling options, then you will also need to know that their gamma will also be much more sensitive than it would be with more traditional options. This means that if you are planning to short options, then a relatively small move overall can still lead to an out-of-the-money option entering in-the-money very quickly.

Weekly options are also known to require a good deal more micromanaging of risk. Without taking the time to size your trades and guarantee your profits properly, you will find that your available trade balance disappears quickly. Furthermore, all of your trades' implied volatility is going to much higher than it would have been otherwise due to the time frame you are dealing with. Near term, options are always going to be more open to large price swings as well.

## Buying Weekly

Because you are always going to have much less time when it comes to turning a profit with a weekly option, your timing for when to move on a specific decision needs to be much more precise than it would otherwise have to be. If you choose poorly at either strike selection, time frame, or price direction, you can easily find yourself paying for a generally worthless option.

You will also need to consider your level of acceptable risk as the option will be cheaper per unit, but you will need to purchase more in a week than you otherwise would.

It is also important to avoid making naked calls or puts when trading weekly as these typically work out to be lower probability trades as a whole. If you have a bias regarding the direction you want your trades to move in, then using a debit spread or structured trade is generally preferred.

## Selling Weekly

Selling reliably for the long-term can generate steady profits if done properly. It only works this way if you are defining your profits upfront, which means it is important always to know what your options are worth to prevent you from selling yourself short. Selling trades weekly will make it easier to collect the full premium if they guess correctly while still leaving you exposed to unmitigated losses if you choose poorly, which requires an extra margin.

The ideal types of the underlying stock to use for these types of trades will be lower priced as they each ultimately consume a smaller amount of your total buying power. This also means it is easier to move forward on trades with lots of implied volatility as it is more likely to revert to the mean in the allotted time.

As a rule, selling a put in the short-term is always better than selling a call as it tends to generate an overall higher return in the shorter period.

## Spreads

Spreads are a great way of making a profit in the weekly market. The overall level of implied volatility will be much higher in the weekly market than in the monthly variation, so the spread can help you when you find yourself dealing with an unexpected directional change quickly enough that you can actually do something about it. Selling an option against a long option will naturally decrease the role volatility plays in the transaction. The best point to use the debit spread will be near the current price, providing you with a 1 to 1 risk and reward ratio.

## Intraday Trades

While options are frequently left out of day trading strategies, this trend is slowly changing. Traders are slowly but surely realizing that they can apply many standard day trading techniques to successfully sell and buy options.

## Intraday Trading Challenges

When attempting to day trade options, you will likely run into some unique challenges that you should be able to best with the proper consideration.

Price movement will decrease value more significantly due to the time value naturally associated with options that are only in-the-money so close to their period of expiration.

Remember, while their inherent value is likely to increase along with the underlying stock price, which will be dramatically countered by the time value loss.

The bid-ask spreads are typically going to be wider than they would otherwise be due to the reduced liquidity that you will typically find with the options market. This will frequently vary by as much as 0.5 of a point, which can cut into profits if things move at an inopportune time.

Some types of options are naturally a better fit when it comes to day trading than others. Perhaps the most effective is the near month in-the-money option, which is appropriate for those traders who are a fan of trading stocks with a high level of liquidity. The premium on this type of option is based more closely on its overall value as it is already in-the-money and getting close to its expiration date. If this occurs, the time value drain is decreased dramatically.

This type of option is generally traded most effectively in periods of high volume, resulting in a decrease in the gap between the asking price and bidding price.

## Protective Put

The protective put is a type of option that is useful when you purchase put orders along with shares of the related underlying stock. This is a reliable strategy when the underlying stock is likely to experience a high degree of volatility. It is especially effective when used to purchase the same option throughout the day to capitalize on short bursts of positive movement. It is also useful for providing insurance when purchasing shares of a risky underlying stock as you will always be limited in your potential losses to the price of the options you purchased.

Protective puts are also useful in a strategy known as bottom fishing. It is common for many underlying stocks to regularly break through existing support levels and continue moving down into an entirely new lower trading range. When this occurs, it is in your best interest to seek out the bottom point of the downturn so that you can catch it before it starts moving back up. It is possible for a stock to give off false signs of having hit bottom and buying in at that point will only lead to serious losses. This is where the protective put comes in, however, and limits the possibility for risk substantially.

While models can be used to calculate the likelihood of the bottom of a given trend, they too can be fooled by the exhausted behavior, which can indicate a false bottom. As such, when you feel that a given stock has bottomed out, then you can buy in with a protective put and then be protected regardless of the outcome.

## Directional Options Trading

The most effective directional strategies for intraday options trading are those with the overall highest degree of making it possible to make quick moves time and again. These moves are typically going to occur at specific retracement levels or around breakouts.

Trades that are based around the Fibonacci retracement on the charts for time frames less than ten minutes. Fibonacci retracements can be used to determine reasonable reward/risk levels either by selling a credit spread to the level in question or buying options that are already in-the-money that are likely to experience a bounce at these levels. It is generally going to be in your best interest to look for Fibonacci levels that are likely to overlap at multiple time frames and correspond to the most recent trend experienced by the underlying stock. If you are so inclined, you can also utilize candlestick price patterns as a means of confirming a buy at specific Fibonacci levels.

Alternately, you may find success with oversold or overbought indicators when it comes to range-bound or trendless stocks. You can then sell credit spreads or buy into options already in-the-money and near the current level of resistance and support with tight stops.

It is important to keep in mind that a given stock might not move quickly enough to make these levels worthwhile, so it is important to do your research ahead of time to have a reasonable expectation about the future movement.

Indicators used to signal lower than average volatility, such as Bollinger bands, are especially useful for place trades that you anticipate big moves from. Breakout indicators time, especially for the shorter charts, are also especially useful.

## High Volatility Options Intraday Strategy

Trading volatility by selling options with high volatility, such as credit spreads currently out-of-the-money, will allow you to profit when anticipating a volatility drop. This is a commonly used professional strategy to employ when it comes to earning season or other scenarios where the underlying stock has developed a big price gap. The front-month short-term options will then have an extra-large amount of volatility that makes it easier to generate a positive reward and risk ratio when selling.

# CHAPTER 3

## Swing Trading With Options

The most straightforward way to trade options is to make a bet on the stock market's direction and buy a call or put options accordingly. Most beginning options traders will have to start with this method because more advanced strategies are closed off to beginning options traders. However, that isn't all bad because you should feel for the options market before attempting more complicated trades.

### What Is Swing Trading?

Swing trading is a simple trading philosophy, where the idea is to trade "swings" in market prices. There is nothing special about swing trading in a commonsense kind of way because it's a buy-low and sell-high trading method with stocks. You can also profit from a stock when the price is declining by "shorting" the stock.

So, what distinguishes swing trading from other types of trading and investing? The main important distinction is that swing trading is different from day trading. A day trader will enter their stock position and exit the position on the same trading day. Day traders never hold a position overnight.

Swing traders hold a position at least for a day, which means they will hold their position at a minimum overnight. Then they will wait for an anticipated "swing" in the stock price to exit the position. This time frame can be days to weeks, or out to a few months, maximum.

A swing trader also differs from an investor, since at the most, the swing trader will be getting out of a position in a few months. Investors often put their money in companies they strongly believe in. Alternatively, they are looking to build a "nest egg" over one to three decades or even more.

Swing traders don't particularly care about the companies they buy stock in. They are simply looking to make a short-term profit. So, although swing traders may not be hoping to make an instant profit like a day trader, they will not be hoping for profits from the long-term prospects of a company. A swing trader is only interested in changing stock prices. Even the reasons behind the changes in the stock prices may not be important. So, whether it's Apple or some unknown company, if it is in a big swing in stock prices, the swing trader will be interested.

## Swing Trading Options

Since options are time-limited, they are a natural fit for the concept of swing trading. Although many of the advanced strategies attempt to take out the direction of share price movement from the equation, if you are buying single call or put options to make a profit, then you're behaving at least in a qualitative sense like a swing trader.

Since put options gain in value when stock prices are declining, buying put options is like shorting the stock. It's quite a bit more accessible, however. You must have a margin account to borrow shares from the broker to short stock. Shorting stock's basic idea is to borrow shares from the broker when the stock price is at a relatively high point and sell them. After this, the trader will wait for the share price to drop. When the share price is low enough to make a profit, the trader will buy the shares back and return them to the broker.

Of course, shorting stock using options is far easier. The reason is you never have to buy the stock to make a profit from the declining price. You profit from the prices of put options, which will increase as the stock price goes down.

## Going Long on a Stock

If you believe that the price of a stock will rise, you want to buy call options. So, call options to represent the most straightforward or commonsense way to trade options. You are betting on that stock when you buy a call option. Another way to say this is that you are bullish on the stock.

A good way to go about trading options is to pick a few companies and limit yourself to trading them. The reason is that you are going to have to be paying attention to the markets, company news, and general financial news for any option that you invest in. You will not be able to stay on top of things and find yourself getting caught up in losing trades if you spread yourself too thin.

The best approach is to keep your trading limited in scope to know what is going on. That doesn't mean you only trade a single call option; you might trade many of them on the same stock.

There are two ways to go about swing trading options. The first way is to look for ranging stocks that are trapped in between support and resistance. Then you can trade call and put options that move with the swings. So, the idea of this type of trading is very simple. First, you need to study a stock of interest and determine the price levels of support and resistance. Then, when the price drops to the support level, you buy call options.

Now hold them until the price goes back up near resistance. It can be a good idea to exit your trades before the price gets to resistance so that you don't end up losing some of your potential profits if the price reverses before you get rid of the options.

Trend trading call options can also be very lucrative. In this case, you are looking for significant news and developments related to the stock or even the economy at large. For example, when a company announces that it had big profits, this can be an opportunity to earn money with call options, as the price will go up by large amounts as people start snapping up the stock. When trading in this fashion, you're going to need to know how to spot trend reversals. The idea is the same when you identify a trend in the making, buy call options, and then ride the trend until you are satisfied with the level of profit and sell the options.

Again, it can't be emphasized too much. You always need to take time to decay into account when trading options. So, remember that with each passing day, your options are going to lose value automatically.

Check theta to find out how much value they are going to lose. Other factors overwhelm time decay in the short term.

A big opportunity with call options is trading on index funds. SPY, which we mentioned earlier, is one of the top choices for trading call options. In the case of SPY, you will be paying attention to overall economic news to look for opportunities. Any information related to the economy at large can cause large moves with this index fund. This includes changes in interest rates (or even leaving them the same when that is what the market would prefer), announcements of GDP growth rates, changes in trade policy, or the release of jobs numbers. One of the best things about SPY options is that they are extremely liquid, making it very easy to get in and out of your trades. You can also trade many other index funds, tracking virtually anything financial.

**Shorting Stock Using Put Options**

Put options may be one of the most powerful tools available to the individual trader. To earn profits from shorting stock, you have to be a big player in the market. That means you have to get a margin account and have enough financial resources that you can borrow large numbers of shares from the broker. Remember that to earn profits from shorting stock, and you'll have to be shorting 100 shares or more of stock to make money.

With put options, you can leverage the stock through the option. By investing in put options, you get control of the stock and earn profits from the stock's price movements without actually having to buy shares. A single put option might cost $30, $100, or $400, but you will control 100 shares.

Some traders hope to profit by selling the shares when they buy put options. Still, most traders want to get into a put option early when a downward trend in stock price is expected and then sell the put option for a profit when stock prices have declined. The same basic things to look for apply, except you'll be doing it in reverse. So, you can trade put options for profits when stocks are ranging. In this case, you start the trade by purchasing put options when stock prices are relatively high, at the resistance level. Then you hold your put options until prices drop down again to support and sell them for a profit.

Likewise, for an options trader, downward trends in stock prices are just as nice as upward trends. When a downward trend is developing, you invest in Put options and then sell them when the stock price has dropped enough such that you are taking an acceptable profit. As with call options, traders using put options will need to learn about signals that indicate trend reversals to have some quantitative tools to help them make solid trades.

Remember there are no guarantees on the options market. When trading options, we are looking for probabilities. This means that you can expect to have some losing trades, and the goal is to be profitable overall without worrying about specific trades.

Swing traders use tools that help them estimate changes in the direction of stock market prices. Some of these tools are more qualitative and involve spotting particular chart patterns that usually indicate a trend reversal is coming. You can think of these tools more in the sense of being rules of thumb or even the art of trading.

# CHAPTER 4

## Understanding Trading Orders

As a trader, you will need a broker through whom you will place, buy, or sell orders for any asset. You can decide whether you will buy or sell any stock and then place an order accordingly on your online trading platform.

Usually, exchanges use a bid and ask process for fulfilling orders placed by traders. This means that there must be a buyer and seller to complete a single order, and they both should agree on the price. For example, if a trader wants to buy a stock at X price, a seller must be willing to sell that stock at the same price. No transaction can occur unless a buyer and a seller agree at the same price.

In stock markets, the price moment is directed by a struggle between the bid and ask prices. These prices keep constantly changing. As trading orders get filled, the price levels also keep changing, reflected in the technical charts.

While day trading, one must keep in mind this bid and ask process because this will determine at what price the order will be executed. When markets are moving slowly, the price change is also slow, and one can wait to get the trading orders filled at the desired price. However, when markets are highly volatile and see big up or down moves within split seconds, the order may get filled at a higher than expected rate.

This can cause losses to day traders as the price changes quickly and can reverse by the time their orders are filled.

Different markets have different methods of matching buyers' and sellers' prices. These methods are called trading mechanisms. The two types of trading mechanisms are order-driven and quote drove. In markets that use quote driven trading, a constant stream of prices (quotes) is available to traders. These prices are decided by market makers; therefore, these types of trading systems are better suited for over the counter (OTC) markets or dealers.

Exchanges mostly adopt the order-driven trading mechanism. Here, orders are executed when buy orders match with a sell order. In this type of trading mechanism, dealmakers are not involved.

## Mechanism of Trading Orders

In electronic day trading, orders are placed on online trading platforms. These orders are the trader's instructions to the broker or the brokerage firm to buy or sell some security. When you are trading stocks, you place orders to buy or sell a stock fulfilled by the brokerage firm with whom you have a trading account. The ease of electronic trading has given traders the freedom to initiate various types of order, where they can use different restrictions in order conditions. By these restrictions, traders can control the price and time of order execution. Such instructions help increase traders' profits or restrict the losses.

In systems where the trading mechanism is order-driven, traders can also control any specific order's timeline. For example, a trader can place an order which will remain open until its execution. Traders can also place orders that last till the end of the session, or one day, or a specific time.

Understanding how trading orders are placed and how they can impact one's day trading is important because it can affect one profit or loss in day trading. For example, a novice day trader may not be aware of the slippage between the bid and ask prices. It occurs in every trade, and every trader faces it, whether buying, selling, entering a position, or exiting from a position.

This is also called the spread between a bid and ask price. So, when you place an order to buy a stock at $4, the slippage may increase its cost to $4.05 when your order is filled. Likewise, when you exist in any position, you place an order to sell at $3, but the slippage causes it to get filled at $2.98, thus chipping away at some of your profits.

Professional traders advise beginners to stay away from highly volatile market situations because of slippage increases during those choppy moments. For example, on a central bank policy declaration day, stock prices become highly volatile and move with big numbers within seconds. The ordered price and executed price may be different in such a situation, causing financial harm to the day trader. Such big moves may look tempting to day traders from the outside, making them greedy, thinking they can make big profits with such huge price moves. But the reality is, the slippage between the bid and ask price is equally high, and it can change considerably by the time the trading order gets filled or immediately after the order is executed, creating a loss-making situation for the trader.

## Different Types of Trading Orders

Most individual traders use a broker's or dealers' trading platforms to place their trading orders. These platforms provide the facility of placing various types of orders, which are helpful in trade planning. Placing an order on the trading platforms is instructing the brokerage firm to buy or sell a financial asset on behalf of the trader. Based on the execution type, here are some common order types:

## Market Orders

These orders do not have any specific price. A market order is an instruction to the broker to complete the trade at the available price. Because there is no fixed price, these orders almost always get executed unless there is some liquidity problem. Traders use market orders when they want their trades executed quickly, and they are not bothered about the execution price.

These orders are good if there is not much slippage between the bid and ask price. But a big slippage can cause loss to the traders, especially those who day trade options.

## Limit Orders

Traders place limit orders when they want to buy or sell stocks (or other assets) at a specific price. For example, if Apple shares are trading at $220, and traders expect the price to dip low, they can limit order to buy the shares at $219 or lower. It can be used for both buying and selling.

Traders use these orders when trading with technical levels and are sure of price touching those levels. For example, if a trader has bought Apple shares at $220 and thinks it can touch $222, they can place a limit order to sell their shares at that higher price. When the share price reaches that level, their sell order will get executed.

## Stop Orders

These are also known as stop-loss orders and make a part of traders' money management techniques. A stop-loss order can stop the trade from going below a specific price, thus restricting losses for the trader. These orders are used for both buy and sell trades. The price specified in a stop-loss order is called stop price; once that price is reached, the order is executed as a market order.

## Day Order

This order is valid only in the same trading session where it is placed. If the specified price is not achieved by the end of the session, the order is automatically canceled. This saves day traders from carrying forward their orders to the following day.

## Preparations for Placing an Order

When preparing day trading plans and strategies, many day traders forget to pay attention to placing orders for trades. The simple act of placing a trading order can have a big impact on the success of your day trading business.

Successful day traders always prioritize order processing techniques and plan their trades around the stock price they will focus on during the trading. The trading plan itself means planning at what price you will enter a trade, and when you will exit. Online trading platforms provide many methods of placing your orders around your planned trade prices. You can prepare charts of your trade, mark entry and exit points, place orders for both trades together and separately.

A good trading plan always includes trade entry, exit, profit booking, and loss stopping points. The margin trading facility provided by various brokerage firms also includes placing a stop-loss order together with the primary buy or sell order. This ensures that your trade will never suffer a loss beyond a specific price level. Here is an example to illustrate this:

Suppose a trader has bought stock "A" at $10. They are expecting the price to go up, so they will make some profit. However, anything can happen in stock markets, and in case of price reverses, they want to restrict their losses to $3 only. So, they will place a stop-loss order at $7, which is $3 below their buying price.

If the price keeps moving up, the stop-loss order will be kept inactive. In case the stock price falls, nothing will happen till it reaches $7, at which time the stop-loss order will be triggered and automatically sell the stock they have bought.

A stop-loss order ensures that even if the trader is not available to check prices, their position will be safe till a certain price.

Similarly, traders can also use limit orders to exit their positions after earning a profit. Taking the above example, if a trader has bought a stock at $10, they believe that the price will move up to $15; they can place a limit order to sell at $15. When the price reaches its target ($15), it will be automatically executed, and the position will be squared off with a profit of $5.

These examples show that day traders can use different order types for money management and manage the risk and reward ratio. By technical analysis of any stock chart, day traders can find at what price the stock will make a big move and be ready to place their orders near that price level.

## Some Other Order Types

Apart from the basic orders, some other order types are not common but can be used for money management or specific trading strategies.

For example, someday, traders are more active during the market closing hours, as they create trading strategies for the next session. To take advantage of the price movement during the closing hours, they can place "Limit-On-Close" (LOC) orders. As the name shows, it is a limit order and is specified for getting executed when markets close.

As you know, a limit order controls at what price any security will be bought or sold. LOC has an extra parameter of "on close," which adds another condition to this order that it should only get executed if the closing price matches the order's price limit. For this order, both the limit price and the market's closing price are important.

# CHAPTER 5

## Market Environment

While the strategies by themselves will limit your risk and give you rewards according to their risk profiles, the most significant risk is applying the wrong strategy to the wrong market conditions.

No strategy can eliminate the risk of you making a mistake, unfortunately. Like the straddle or strangle, even a neutral strategy will not work if you misread a range for a trend.

Technical and fundamental analysis will help you determine what market conditions are appropriate. Every trader has different perspectives towards technical analysis regarding determining which stocks to operate in. This is because fundamental analysis favors longer timelines, of over 5 years, for investment purposes. While the earnings announcements are important, a fundamentally low valuation doesn't play out over a few months.

Learn some basics about the market environment: namely, what is a trend and what is a range.

## Trends and Ranges

A market is a chaotic place, with several traders vying for dominance over one another. There are countless strategies and time frames in play, and at any point, it is close to impossible to determine who will emerge with the upper hand. In such an environment, how is it then possible to make any money? After all, if everything is unpredictable, how can you get your picks?

Well, this is where thinking in terms of probabilities comes into play. While you cannot get every single bet right, if you get enough right and make enough money on those to offset your losses, you will make money in the long run.

It's not about getting one or two right. It's about executing the strategy with the best odds of winning repeatedly and ensuring that your math works out with regards to the relationship between your win rate and average win.

So, it comes down to finding patterns that repeat themselves over time in the markets. What causes these patterns? Well, the other traders, of course. To put it more accurately, the orders that the other traders place in the market create patterns that repeat themselves over time.

The first step to understanding these patterns is to understand what trends and ranges are. Identifying them and learning to spot them when they transition into one another will give you a massive leg up with your options trading and directional trading.

## Trends

In theory, spotting a trend is simple enough. Look left to right, and if the price is headed up or down, it's a trend. Most of the time, you have countertrend forces operating in the market. It is possible to have long counter-trend reactions within a larger trend, and sometimes, depending on the time frame you're in, and these counter-trend reactions take up most of your screen space.

## Trend vs. Range

The key to deciphering trends is to watch for two things: countertrend participation quality and turning points. Let's tackle countertrend participation first.

## Countertrend Participation

When a new trend begins, the market experiences an extremely imbalanced order flow tilted towards one side. There's isn't much countertrend participation against this seeming tidal wave of with trend orders. Price marches on without any opposition and experiences only a few hiccups.

This is where countertrend traders start testing the trend and see how far back into their trend. While it is unrealistic to expect a full reversal at this point, the correction or pushback quality tells us a lot about the strength distribution between the with and countertrend forces.

Eventually, the countertrend players manage to push so far back against the trend of stalemate results in the market. After all, you need an imbalance for the market to tip one way or another, and balanced order flow will only result in a sideways market.

While all this is going on behind the scenes, the price chart is what records the push and pull between these two forces. Using the price chart, we can anticipate when a trend is coming to an end and how long it could potentially take before it does.

This second factor, which helps us estimate the time it could take, is invaluable from an options perspective, especially if you're using a horizontal spread strategy.

Here's what you look out for to gauge countertrend participation:

- Quality of countertrend candles: Are they strong/weak/have wicks/small-bodied, etc.?
- Several countertrend candles within the movement: Is this changing over time?
- Length of pushbacks: Are the pushbacks increasing in number? Are they lasting for longer?

In all cases, the greater the number of them, the greater the countertrend participation in the market. The closer a trend is to end, the greater the countertrend participation. Thus, the minute you begin to see price move into a large, sideways move with an equal number of buyers and sellers in it, you can be sure that some form of redistribution is going on.

The trend might continue or reverse. Either way, it doesn't matter. What matters is that you know the trend is weak and that now is probably not the time to be banking on-trend strategies.

Starting from the left, we can see that there is close to no countertrend bars, bearish in this case, and the bulls make easy progress. Note the angle with which the bulls proceed upwards.

Then comes the first major correction and the countertrend players push back against the last third of the bull move. Notice how strong the bearish bars are and note their character compared to the bullish bars.

The bulls recover and push the price higher at the original angle and without any bearish presence, which seems odd. This is soon explained as the bears slam price back down, and for a while, it looks as if they've managed to form a V top reversal in the trend, which is an extremely rare occurrence.

The price action that follows is a more accurate reflection of the market's power, with both bulls and bears sharing chunks of the order flow, with overall order flow in the bull's favor but only just. The price here is certainly in an uptrend but looking at the extent of the bearish pushbacks, perhaps we should be on our guard for a bearish reversal. After all, order flow is looking sideways at this point.

So how would we approach an options strategy with the state's chart at the extreme, right? Well, for one, any strategy that requires an option beyond the near month is out of the question, given the probability of it turning. Secondly, looking at the order flow, it does seem to be following a channel.

While the channel isn't very clean if you were aggressive enough, you could consider deploying a collar with the strike prices above and below this channel to take advantage of the price movement. You could also employ some moderately bullish strategies as price approaches the bottom of this channel and figuring out the extent of the bull move is easier thanks to you referencing the channel's top.

As the price moves in this channel, it's all well and good. Eventually, though, we know that the trend must flip. How do we know when this happens?

**Turning Points**

As bulls and bears struggle over who gets to control the order flow, price swings up and down. You will notice that every time price comes back into the 6427–6349 zone, the bulls seem to step in masse and repulse the bears.

This tells us that the bulls are willing to defend this level in large numbers and strength. Given the number of times the bears have tested this level, we can safely assume that bullish strength is a bit weak above this level. However, it is as if the bulls have retreated at this level and are treating this as a last resort for the trend to be maintained.

If this level were to be breached by the bears, it is a good bet that many bulls will be taken out. In martial terms, the largest army of bulls has been marshaled at this level. If this force is defeated, it is unlikely that there will be too much resistance to the bears below this level.

This zone, in short, is a turning point. If price breaches this zone decisively, we can safely assume that the bears have moved in and controlled most of the order flow.

### *Turning Point Breached*

The two horizontal lines mark the decisive turning point zone, and the price touches this level twice more and is repulsed by the bulls. Notice how the last bounce before the level breaks produces an extremely weak bullish bounce, and price caves through this. Notice the strength with which bears breakthrough.

The FTSE was in a longer uptrend on the weekly chart, so the bulls aren't completely done yet. However, as far as the daily timeframe is concerned, notice how price retests that same level but this time around, it acts as resistance instead of support.

For now, we can conclude that if the price remains below the turning point, we are bearishly biased. You can see this by looking at the angle with which bulls push back and the lack of strong bearish participation on the push upwards.

This doesn't mean we go ahead and pencil in a bull move and start implementing strategies that take advantage of the upcoming bullish move. Remember, nothing is for certain in the markets. Don't change your bias or strategy until the turning point decisively breaks.

Some key things to note here are that a turning point is always a major S/R level. It is usually a swing point where many with trend forces gather to support the trend. Don't hang on to older turning points as this will not always be the case.

# CHAPTER 6

## Q&A to Help You Get the Most Out of Trading

### 1. Why Is It Better to Trade in Options Than Other Forms of Investing?

Many benefits come with options trading compared to some of the other investment choices that you can make. To start, you don't have to purchase the underlying asset. With the options contract, you are purchasing the right, but not the obligation, to either purchase or sell the asset at a later time. You get the benefit of making a profit once you decide to exercise this right. But if the trade goes oppositely, you don't have to exercise your right to use the underlying asset, and your losses are often limited to the fee or the deposit that you placed on the trade in the beginning.

### 2. What Are Some of the Ways That I Can Limit My Losses?

We spent some time talking about some of the different ways to limit the number of losses you have. There are several risks with any investment, and you could end up losing money along the way. Even those who have worked in the options market for some time may experience losses on occasion.

These are the things that you can do to help limit these losses a bit, including:

- Make a plan and stick to it.

- Know your stop-loss points.

- Invest in something you know.

- Never risk capital than you can afford to lose.

- Learn how to keep the emotions out of the trade.

### 3. What Are the Differences Between Puts and Calls?

This will refer to the right that you have when it comes to working with your options trading. When we talk about a call option, it means that you have the right to buy the underlying asset. But when we are talking about the put option, we are talking about having the right to sell that underlying asset. Ensure that you know each of these and that your plan is set up to work with the right one before you start.

## 4. What Assets Can I Trade-In?

Options trading can technically be done on any asset that you want. Remember that with options, you will purchase the right, but not the obligation, to purchase the underlying asset. But the underlying asset can be almost anything that you want. With that said, most of the time, the underlying asset will be some stock option. Ensure that you research the different types of assets that can be done in options and determine which one is the best for you.

## 5. What Are Some of the Characteristics of a Kind Options Trader?

As an options trader, you need to be careful with your investment and be sure that you are taking all the necessary precautions before entering the market. A good investment trader, in options and in other forms of investing, will have some of the following:

- **Capital to invest.** You won't even be able to talk to the broker until you can bring some money to the table. It is preferable if you have some extra money set to the side that isn't earmarked for some other purpose in your life.

- **Some time.** You must have at least a little bit of time to ensure that you will be able to look at the charts and watch your trade to make sure you are successful.

- **Research abilities.** The investments that you take are going to need some research behind them. If you can do your research, hear about the news surrounding your trades, and look through many charts, you will do better with options trading.

- **Controlling emotions.** If you aren't able to control your own emotions, then you are going to fail. For those who let their emotions take over all the time, finding another investment opportunity is a much better option to help you do well. If you are levelheaded and can pay attention to your investment without losing your cool, options are a great choice.

### 6. Can I Trade-In Options Even if the Market Is Going Down?

Unlike some of the other investment opportunities that you may run into, you can trade-in options even if the market is in a downward trend at the time. You can trade-in options even if the market is stagnant, volatile, and whether it is going up or down. There are various strategies that you can choose no matter how the market is doing at the time. This is one of the biggest reasons that people choose to go with options as their investment vehicle. They can make some good profits from their work, no matter what the market is doing around them.

## 7. Is it Safe to Invest in Options?

Compared to some of the other choices you have for investing, especially with day trading and swing trading, options trading is much safer. Many investors choose to go with options trading to help protect themselves from any downturns that could harm their other investments. With that said, there is still an element of risk that can come with investing in options, and you should still make sure that there is some plan in place before you decide to enter into the market. Other risks come with using this form of investing, and you have to be careful and stick with your plan if you want to see success.

# CHAPTER 7

## Financial Freedom

While there are many things that you may dream of accomplishing in your life, you will find that almost everyone is interested in gaining financial freedom. Being free financially means that you can maintain the lifestyle that you want without a regular paycheck. It is like having a retirement where you can live comfortably and maybe go out, and have some fun without worrying about stretching yourself too thin.

There are a lot of ways that come with gaining financial freedom. It is not a single point in time, but rather four stages that will lead you to this. The four stages of financial freedom that you should follow include:

### No Freedom

Everyone is going to start the journey in the same place. You will rely on your monthly paycheck during this stage. You will see that a job and the reliable income stream that it provides are required so that you can pay the bills. If something happened to your income and you no longer received that paycheck, your savings would be depleted quickly, and you may end up defaulting on your monthly expenses. It is the starting point to be financially free, and you will work from here.

## Temporary Freedom

You will still need your income regularly in this second stage, but you can spend less than what you earn. You can then turn the extra over into a pool of savings. You want to get into this stage to build up good savings; otherwise, you will end up working forever because your lifestyle will depend on all the money you earn. As you start to save some of your income, even if that amount is small initially, consider investing your savings into a diversified investment that will provide you with a stream of income when it grows. Or, you have the possibility of starting a business on the side so that you can create a second source of income.

You will find that your freedom is going to grow along with your savings. Over time, you will have saved enough money so that you are comfortable. You may decide to take some time to travel for a year, go back to school, start your own business, switch jobs, or do other things that would be hard if you worked a full-time job. These are significant changes in your life, but these are not permanent changes. The freedom that comes with this stage is going to be temporary. Your income will usually exceed your expenses with this one, and you will not be able to remain free for too long.

## Permanent Freedom

When you get to the third stage, the non-employment income you make will be higher than your total expenses. You would be able to quit working your regular job and still have enough from your business or your investment that you are still able to pay all your bills. Have a reliable income that keeps coming in so that you can enjoy life and gain permanent freedom, not one that will be gone quickly.

If you have a side business, you will still put in some labor to make it work. You will still be trading your time for money. But it is much different compared to what you would do working for someone else. The side job that you take over should represent your passion, and be something that you enjoy doing. It means that while you may be working at a side job, you will enjoy it, and you will feel like you are free.

Having fulfillment is the entire point of financial freedom. It's all about having the independence to choose how your daily routine will go, and it will allow you to design a better life while being able to spend your energy, money, and time in a more meaningful way. This could include investing, starting a side business, or doing something else that you enjoy that brings in money.

## Luxurious Freedom

This is a stage that is not going to be achieved by very many people. This is where you can have enough of a passive income that you can spend it freely. Your income will exceed the expenses that you have by a large margin to live the lifestyle that you would like without putting in much more work.

It is a challenging time to accomplish. You will have to work hard at your passive income, and perhaps have a few different sources so that you can earn enough to make this work. You have a choice. You can choose to get your passive income to a point where you can cover the bills and then stop, and hope you don't go backward. Or you can work a bit longer and end up with the luxurious freedom that we just talked about.

Do you want financial freedom?

There are three main questions that you should ask yourself. These include:

- Are you happy with the lifestyle that you have right now?

- Have you found a job that has good work to life balance?

- Do you enjoy the job that you do and enjoy the purpose of your daily routine?

These are hard questions that you have to answer, but they will help you determine your thoughts about gaining financial freedom. There are three categories that you can split these into. First, you have to check whether your work is meaningful. Some individuals like their jobs and see no reason why they should stop working. This is just fine because you can work while also being financially free.

The second category is that work is okay for you. You do not particularly enjoy the job, but it is something that you do because it is something that you don't completely despise, which will pay the bills.

If you are in this second situation, your preferred level of freedom financially should be inversely related to the amount of disdain that you have for your work. It is up to you to work harder to increase the amount of savings you have to have more control, and even change careers if you would like.

And finally, you could fall into the third group where you find work boring and somewhat terrible. For this group, financial freedom should be high on your priority list. If you hate the job you are in, it should be easy to make sacrifices to find a way to escape. This would include working a second job, moving somewhere with a lower cost of living, and cutting unnecessary expenses. Spend this time saving all the money that you can so that you can change jobs.

By focusing on this freedom, the perspective that you have is likely to change. You will go from sludging through many more years at a job you don't like to design the life that you would like to have. Remember that you will be more likely to see success when you can devote all your energy, time, and money to that goal.

During this point, time, rather than money, is the most valuable asset that you have. If your time at that job makes you miserable, it is time to save money to quit your job.

# CHAPTER 8

## Habits and Mindset of The Financially Free

Financial freedom is coming from within you. It is why you need to invest in yourself. You need to take care of your mind and body because it is where the energy to get financial freedom comes from. Our self is what has the conscious and subconscious mind.

Certain things in your life will need to change in your life to make sure you are communicating positively with your subconscious mind.

### Positive Thinking

As much as having positive thoughts seems easy, it is not. As human beings, we have the tendency always to think the worst of any situation. Our minds are geared towards seeing the faults rather than seeing the right things. Most times in our lives, we have missed out on many good things because we're focused on the wrong things. Be sure that your mind will always look for what you are used to. If you are used to seeing the wrong and harmful side of every situation, then when things happen, the negative results will hit you first. And most of the time, you will be so consumed by these negative thoughts that you will not take time to review the positive results.

## Habits

If you have bad habits like always thinking negatively and procrastinating, then you need to change immediately. The good thing about a bad habit is it can be replaced with a good one. It will be easy to replace bad habits if you are willing to work towards replacing them. The best way to replace these bad habits is to start practicing good habits regularly. With time you will find yourself practicing these good habits as a norm.

Cultivate good habits like:

- Having positive thoughts about yourself, your money, and your work

- Setting goals for yourself

- Being accountable for your actions

- Learning to engage with people well

- Working on getting results and not just for the sake of it

- Living within your means

- Having savings

Remember that these habits are what the subconscious mind is going to record. Many financially free people are described to be people with good habits. They always have habits that set them apart and make them attain their success. You will find all of them have goals and always think positively.

They have taught themselves and commissioned their minds and bodies only to perform these tasks, and never allow themselves or anyone around them to pick up bad habits because they know their impact.

## Self-discipline

Being self-disciplined means having control over your life to do what you are required to do. At the time, it should be done whether you feel like doing it or not. To achieve good results in life, you need to be disciplined. Cultivating good habits and having good thoughts requires a lot of discipline.

You are also working towards financial freedom, which means you will be handling a lot of money. If you are not disciplined, you will squander all the money and have even more debts than before. You know how life works. The more money you make, the more needs you get. Most times, the needs increase because we want to change our lifestyle.

As much as our lifestyles change, we need the discipline to take care of the money we are making and the assets we are acquiring.

Discipline will help you stick to your goals and make sure you achieve them. When you look at people with poor mindsets, you see no discipline in what they do. They do not meet their goals and deadlines, and they are not accountable for the things they do.

But people with a wealthy mindset are very disciplined. You will see them cultivating good habits in their lives, and they live by them. They set reasonable goals and deadlines, and are disciplined to make sure they achieve them.

Their minds are set towards achieving something, and they know that discipline will keep them on track. Most of these people, when asked, will tell you that they have a daily schedule that they follow, and no minute of their day is wasted.

## Knowledge

People geared toward financial freedom are always looking to learn something new. They are aware that the world is dynamic, and things change from time to time. So, they make sure they always know what the new version of something is. They always want to know what other methods they can employ to make their business successful.

As they keep learning and upgrading, their subconscious mind will register their interest in what they are doing, and they will be successful in it.

Poor mindset people will always stick to one way of doing things. They are lazy, so they do not want to think of better ways of changing the system they have in place. Investing in better equipment, and personnel to them is a lot of work that is money-wasting. They remain with the same methods even after they are outdated, and with time their businesses no longer produce quality products that consumers are looking for.

## Invest in Your Health

You cannot enjoy your financial freedom if your health is failing. Do not lose yourself in your work and compromise your health. Donkey work is not what will get you to financial freedom. It is all in mind. How you set your mind will determine your success. You can be working hard, and your mindset is in the wrong place, so you do not achieve results.

You need to take enough rest and be physically active. Watch what you eat and what information you consume. Do not allow yourself to be stressed. Go for regular check-ups, and follow the directives of the doctor. Financial freedom requires a lot of energy. Having a positive mindset also requires a lot of energy. Always look out for your health so you can have this energy you need to grow.

## Be Your Own Cheerleader

Cheer yourself on as you go. When you start new projects as you progress in achieving a goal, each time you have a win when pitching ideas, cheer yourself on. Congratulate yourself when you have won, no matter how big or small.

Be your biggest supporter. This is going to help you tune a positive mindset. Your senses will be helping you to progress in your life. The subconscious mind will pick on your enthusiasm and manifest success in your life. It will help when you see yourself as a winner in your own eyes.

People with poor mindsets often tend to be their number one hater. When things do not go well, they think things like, "I knew I wasn't going to make it," or "I am not good enough to do that." They hinder their growth themselves with their own thoughts and actions, and the subconscious mind manifests their thought failure.

## Be Goal-Oriented

Always set goals for yourself. Goals will help you know what you want to achieve. Without goals, you will be working blindly because you will not know what you want to have achieved by the end of a specific time or project. The best way to set goals is to have long-term and short-term goals.

Be assured that your subconscious mind is going to note your goals. It is going to feed on your conscious mind what you are planning to achieve. Then it will begin to manifest these goals in your life. They will come to pass one after another.

But it will be hard to achieve anything if you have no idea what you are working towards. Setting goals will help you envision what you want, and the subconscious will record it. Your mindset will also be set towards achieving the goals.

There is no good feeling like that of achieving goals. See salespeople congratulating themselves and celebrating when they meet their weekly or monthly goals. Meeting their goals means earning more money because of commissions and other benefits. Now imagine how much you can achieve if you set reasonable goals and work towards them. Your path to financial freedom will be clearer now that you visualize how you want to get there.

## Have a Plan

A plan will help you organize your thoughts, and know precisely how you will manage your financial freedom. You are going to avoid being confused and stagnant, not knowing what move to make next.

By the time you are making a plan, you will already have your goals written out. The plan is your execution strategy. How you intend to achieve your goals. With a plan, you will also have the opportunity to visualize how you are going to achieve your goals. You can map out your strategies and see how you want to work. All this will be registered in your subconscious mind. And with the right mindset, you will achieve them. Be good and generous to people

You may have the right attitude towards getting your financial freedom, but you will not reach far if you are not good to people. No man is an island. You will need people to hold your hand and help you on this journey. They could be the people that will help you with the finances you need. Or the people that will help you produce and sell your products. Either way, it is essential to be fair and generous to all of them.

Always have a generous heart. Have the conviction in you to help others succeed. This goodwill is not going to go unnoticed. It is like you are sowing a good seed in your life, and it will reap good things.

## Be Accountable

Always account for everything you do. Account for money used to fund a project, money received from salaries and assets. Be a good manager. Know that you will be blessed with more when your subconscious notes that you are working at managing the little that you have.

Find someone that has achieved financial freedom or is working towards it. These are the best people to help you because they know what you need to work on to attain financial freedom.

## Organization

Organize your thoughts and your plans. This is the best way to make sure you are not confusing your subconscious mind. You will not have different thoughts and ideas that are not in a particular order. It is good to organize them by writing them down. When you are looking at them, your mind will now pick up the points. Before, when they are just thoughts, they may sound and feel technical. But when you write them down, you will be able to understand them better. And you will not forget about an idea or a goal you had.

You can write them in your journal, diary, or vision board. Draw diagrams, use different colors, have graphs. Make your work exciting and colorful, so when you look at it, you get excited. The subconscious mind will note this excitement. It will change your mindset to your plans and goals. They will stop feeling bulky and unachievable, and you will have confidence that you can do it. But make sure the thoughts flow from what you want to achieve first to last.

# CHAPTER 9

## Stocks Vs Options

There is a big difference between options and stock.

Stock represents partial ownership of the company, implying that you are usually a part of the company when you purchase a stock. On the other hand, options trading is merely any ownership of a particular company; it is a contract involving a trader and another party that allows the trader to purchase or sell a certain amount of stock at a specific price within a particular period. The market may be so volatile, but the strike prices are so high, and when the market activities are depicted to be calm, the strike prices may eventually be so down.

The following are some of the major differences between options and stock:

- Options tend to expire, as detailed by the expiration dates. While stocks are much long-lasting since they are properties of the company and bear no expiration dates. Therefore, stock trading is likely to happen for a longer period as compared to stock trading.
- Options derive the actual value from the value of the other assets involved during options trading. In contrast, stocks have a definite actual value that is fully recognized by the company in question.

- In the options trading activities, traders have the full rights of the value amount. On the other hand, stock trading gives the traders full ownership of the property involved during trading activities.

- In options trading, the market predictability does not necessarily depend on the rates of supply and demand levels than stock trading. With this in mind, the options trader is unlikely to predict what happens to the market, but he/she can, however, check on the market's volatility.

- Options are much cheaper than stock. Money is so fundamental in trading and is always the biggest motivation in any trading activity. Options are less expensive since the trader gets to acquire 100 shares of the equity during trading. Moreover, the cost of grasping an option contract is much cheaper as compared to purchasing and the underlying stock, and the trader acquires more amounts of benefits as compared to stock trading.

- Options are usually a great leverage tool in maximizing the amounts of profits gained during a particular trading period compared to stock trading. This is evident in the collection of various amounts of premiums during the issuance of contracts hence increasing the amounts of profits collected in options trading compared to stock trading.

- Options trading is much good at flexibility compared to stock trading, as evident in its tactical operations that frequently happen in various trading activities. Traders can make smaller investments that lead to good amounts of profits, and fewer risks involved during a particular period.

On the other hand, stock trading calls for good investments with multiple amounts of risks over an unspecified period.

- Another point is that options have a great chance of limiting the risks that are likely to be involved during trading than stock trading, where risk is pretty much unlimited during the unspecified period of trading.

- Options trading can better for you if your timing is okay, and as an options trader, you will be able to acquire larger amounts of profits during the contract compared to when you would be involved in options trading.

- Options trading allows a particular option trader to bet where the market will not go, an activity that is not allowed in stock trading. The advantage of this opportunity is that there are higher chances of success than betting on where the market will go.

# CHAPTER 10

## Basics Of Options

The call option offers the holder the right to purchase the stock, and the put option offers the holder the right to sell the stock. See the call option as a down payment for a futuristic purpose.

### Example of a Call Option

A prospective homeowner sees the rise of new development. That person may want the right to buy a new house in the future but will only want to exert that right once other developments in the area have been made.

The prospective home buyer will gain from the option of buying or not. Imagine they can purchase a call option from the developer to purchase the home at probably $400,000 at whatever point in the following three years. Oh, they can, because it's a non-refundable deposit. Usually, the developer wouldn't offer such an option for free. The prospective home buyer has to contribute a down-payment to keep that right locked.

As far as an option is concerned, this cost is referred to as the premium. It is the price of an option contract. In the home example, the deposit may be $20,000 paid by the purchaser to the developer. Assume two years have gone by, and new developments are underway, and zoning has been approved. The home buyer exerts the option and decides to buy the home at $400,000 because that's the contract he has bought.

The market value of the home may have been doubled to $800,000. The buyer pays $400,000 because the down payment is locked at a pre-determined price. In an alternative scenario, let's say zoning approval doesn't come through till year four. This is one year after this option has expired. Now the home buyer has to pay the market price since the contract is expired already. In either case, the developer will keep the initial $20,000 collected.

## Example of Put Option

If you own your home, you're probably familiar with buying homeowner insurance. Think of the put option as an insurance policy. A homeowner purchases a homeowner's policy to protect his home from damage. They pay a certain amount known as the premium for a particular period, let's say a year. The policy has a face value and provides security to the insurance holder if the home is destroyed.

What if your asset was a stock or an index investment instead of a home? Comparably, if an investor needs insurance on his index portfolio (S&P 500), he can buy put options. The investor might fear that the bear market is close and may not be willing to lose more than 10 percent of its long position in the S&P 500 Index. If the S&P 500 is currently trading at $2,500, he/she may buy a put option that gives the right to sell the index at $2,250, for instance, at any point during the next two years.

If the market collapses by 20% (500 points on the index) in six months, he or she would have made 250 points by being willing to sell the index at $2250 while trading at $2000, a total loss of just 10%. Even though the market hits zero, the loss will only be 10% if this option is retained. Again, buying the option will have a cost (the premium) and, if the market does not collapse during that time, the maximum loss on the option is only the premium that was spent.

# CHAPTER 11

## The Time Value

Every options contract has a time value, but it's also subject to time decay. Time value is the option's price that comes from the amount of time remaining until the option expires. The time or extrinsic value is not exact and can change based on the option's price relative to the market. To give an example, the more an option goes into the money, the less it's impacted by time decay. But one thing is certain; all options are impacted by time decay. Simply put, this means that the price of the options will decline as time passes.

For sellers of options contracts, time decay is their best friend. That makes it more likely the options will expire worthlessly, and the option won't be exercised.

For buyers of options contracts, time is your enemy. You are looking to profit before time runs out. Whether or not you can do so will depend on whether or not the option is in the money or not.

Also, remember that time value is also called extrinsic value. The option also has intrinsic value. This is pricing derived from the underlying stock. Properties that can influence it include price and its properties like volatility. Extrinsic value comes from the outside.

When options are sold, they all have time value. They have time value because the more time there is until the option expires; the probability is increased that the option can go in the money at some point. And that is when the option is worth something. But as time passes and the expiration date starts getting closer and closer, the less time there is for a stock to make a move. Of course, stocks make significant moves over short periods and even over a day or two, but the shorter the time left to expiration, the lower the probability that this will happen.

Let's look at a few examples. It helps hold variables constant and isolate the variable you are trying to learn about to understand how things work. That is a fictitious example, but once you understand how things work by examining them in isolation, you will be far more capable of understanding how the pricing of real options is changing and why.

We will begin with a stock with a $100 share price with 30 days left before expiration in the examples. We will set the implied volatility to 15%.

Let's consider an option which is at the money. If the strike price was $100, the call and the put for this option are priced at $1.78 and $1.76, respectively (remember to multiply by 100 to get the actual price you would have to pay to buy the option or the price you'd get selling the option).

Now let's see how time decay impacts the option prices. Simply moving to 20 days left to expiration, we find that the price of the call and put options have declined to $1.45 and $1.44, respectively. Both have declined because the strike is equal to the market price, and the only thing impacting the price of the option is time decay. With only 20 days left to expiration, the options have less time value. At this point, 100% of the option value is extrinsic, determined by time value.

Now let's shift the clock again to 10 days to expiration. Now the call option has dropped to $1.03, and the put option is $1.02. At seven days to expiration, the call option is $0.86, and the put option is $0.85. Moving to 3 days to expiration, the call option and put option are both priced at $0.56. Finally, one day to expiration, the call and put option are both worth $0.32.

Time decay works exponentially. In practice, it means that the closer you get to the expiration date, the faster the option decays' extrinsic or time value.

But let us consider what would happen if the option went in the money, right at the last moment. First, consider what would happen if the stock price went up to $102 a share. In that case, it means the call option is "in the money." We find that the price of the call jumps to $2.00. The put would be virtually worthless.

On the other hand, the stock price dropped by $2; instead, it would be the put that would be priced at $2.00, and the call would be virtually worthless.

Time decay always impacts options, except toward the end, the intrinsic value (see below) can overwhelm it.

The degree to which it does depends on how far in the money the option price has moved.

Now let us consider an in the money option. First, we'll consider a put option, and we'll say the stock price is $98 a share, with a strike price of $100. With 30 days left to expiration, the put option is $2.91. The call option is $0.94. So, the call option, which is out of the money, is a comparative bargain, and if you are expecting the stock to rise over the next 30 days, it could be a good move to buy that call option.

If nothing else changes at 20 days to expiration (the stock price of $98, strike price of $100), the call option is priced at $0.65, and the put option is $2.64. It is an important note, so even though the put option is in the money, we see a price decline. This happens as a result of lost time value.

At ten days to expiration, the prices of the call and put have dropped to $0.31 and $2.30, respectively. At seven days, the put option is $2.19, and the call option is $0.20. Finally, with two days left to expiration, the put option is $2.02, while the call option is a mere $0.02.

The same thing would happen to a call option in the money if everything, but time decay was held constant. The call option will still have some value before expiration, but it would steadily lose it. If the stock price were $102, and we had a call option that has a strike set at $100, the option price on the following remaining time frames: 30, 20, 10, 7, and 3 days to expiration, would be: $2.98, $2.68, $2.33, $2.21, and $2.05.

The takeaway lesson is that the time value of an option always decreases.

# CHAPTER 12

## Time Decay

If an option is valued so that it is the same as the share price, or if it is out of the money, time decay will have a significant influence over the value of an option at any given time. For an option that can be said to be in the money, the influence of time decay will be much less. The closer you get to the expiration date; the time value exerts less influence on the option's overall price. In that case, it's going to be more influenced by implied volatility and the underlying share price.

Options prices are determined in part by the price of the underlying stock. But options prices are also influenced by the time left to expiration and some other factors. We will go over all the different ways that the price of a given option can change, and what will be behind the changes. It has 0 intrinsic values if an option can be the same as the market pricing or not be ideal.

It would have to be priced in the money to have any intrinsic value.

- For a call option, if the market price is lower than the strike price or the same, the option will have no pricing at all from the intrinsic value. Once the share price is higher than the price used to trade shares via the option, it will have intrinsic value.

- For a put option, once the share price is at or above the strike price, it will have 0 intrinsic values. If the share price is lower than the strike price, then it will have some value from the stock. This is called intrinsic value.

Even when an option is at or out of the money, the underlying stock price has some influence that can change the value of the option. The amount of influence that the item's market price known as the stock has on the price of the option is given by a quantity called delta. You can read the value for delta by looking at the data for any option you are interested in trading.

For call options, a decimal number ranging from 0 to 1 is given and a negative value for put options. It's given as a negative value for put options because this reflects the fact that if the stock price is found to increase, the price of a put option will be reduced. In contrast, if the stock price declines, the value of the put option will increase. It's an inverse relationship, and thus, the delta is negative for put options.

To understand how this will play out, let's look at a specific example. Suppose that we have a $100 option. That is, the strike price is set to $100. If the underlying stock price is $105, the delta for the call option is 0.77.

That means that if the dollar value of the stock increases by $1, the option's value will rise by approximately 77 cents. This is a per-share price change. So, for the option that you are trading, there are 100 underlying shares. So, a 77-cent price rise would increase the value of the option by $77.

For a put option with the same strike price, the option would be out of the money because the share price is higher than the strike price. In this case, for the put option, the delta is given as -0.23. That means that the put option would lose approximately $23 if the share price went up by $1. On the other hand, if the share price dropped by $1, the put option would gain $23.

The intrinsic value of the call option described in this theoretical exercise would be $5 per share. The option's total cost would be $6.06 per share, reflecting the fact that the call option has $1.06 in extrinsic value. In contrast, the put option has zero intrinsic value. It has almost the same extrinsic value, however, at $1.03.

Mathematical formulas govern option prices, so it's possible to estimate the option price ahead of time. Some many calculators and spreadsheets are available free online for this purpose.

To take an example, at four days to expiration, a $100 strike price on an underlying stock when the market price is set equal to $110 per share will have $10 in intrinsic value with $0.56 in extrinsic value and a total price per share of $10.56. So, the price is heavily weighted to the underlying price of the shares. However, theta is -0.23, meaning that on a per-share basis, the option will lose $0.23 in value at the market open the following day, all other things being equal. Of course, all other things are not equal, and changes in share price and implied volatility may wipe that out or add to it.

The important thing to do is check theta every afternoon so you can estimate what the cost is going to be for holding the option overnight. Time decay is an exponential phenomenon, so it decays faster the closer you get to the expiration date. The trader's important path is knowing when other factors are going to be more important than time decay. You are not only going to sell off your option because it's going to lose value from time decay the following morning.

You will also see the risk-free rate quoted for an option. This is the interest rate that you could earn on an ideal safe investment. Generally speaking, this would be the interest you could earn from a 10-year U.S. treasury throughout the option. In regular times, this is an essential factor to consider. Rising interest rates (that is significantly rising) can lower the value of options. In recent years, interest rates have been very low, and changes in interest rates have been small and very conservative. So, at present, at least, this is not something to worry about.

# CHAPTER 13

## Volatility Strategies

As an options trader, you need to learn about the variables that can affect an option's price and the INS, and outs of implementing the right strategy. A stock trader who is familiar and good with predicting future stock price movement might think that shifting to options trading is easy, but it's not. There are three changing parameters that an options trader must deal with: the underlying stock's price, the time factor, and volatility.

The price of an option is also called the premium, and the pricing is per share. The option seller receives the premium, which gives the buyer any right that comes with the option. The buyer is the one paying the premium to the seller, and they can exercise this right or allow the option to expire without any worth in the end. The buyer is obliged to pay the premium whether the option is exercised or not, which means the seller will keep the premium, in the end, no matter what.

Let's have a simple example. A buyer paid a seller for purchasing rights to stock ABC for 100 shares, and a strike price at $60. The contract expires on June 19. If the option position becomes profitable, the option will be exercised by the buyer. If it does not seem to bear profit, the buyer can just let the contract expire. The seller then keeps the premium.

There are two sides to the premium of an option: its intrinsic and time value. You can compute an option's intrinsic value by getting the difference between the strike price and the stock price. For the call option, it is the stock price minus the strike price. For the put option, it is the strike price minus the stock price.

To value an option, at least theoretically, you will need to consider multiple variables such as the underlying stock price, volatility, exercise price, time to expiration, and interest rate. These factors will provide you with a reasonable estimate of the fair value of an option that you can incorporate into your strategy for maximum gains.

The value of puts and calls are affected by underlying stock price movements straightforwardly. That means when the price of a stock rises, there should be a corresponding rise in call value as well since you can purchase the underlying stock at a reduced price compared to the market's, while there is a price decrease input.

There should be an increase in the value of put options when the stock price dives, and a decrease in call options since the put option holder can sell the stock at above-market prices. This pre-set price you can sell, or buy is called the option's strike price or its exercise price. If the option's strike price gives you the advantage of selling or buying the stock at a cost that gives you immediate profit, that option is considered 'in the money.'

Volatility affects most investment forms to some degree, and as an options trader, you should be familiar with this element and how it affects options pricing. Volatility is the tendency of something to fluctuate or change significantly. In general investment, volatility refers to the rate a financial instrument price rises or falls.

A low volatility financial instrument has a relatively stable price. Conversely, a high volatility financial instrument is prone to dramatic price changes, either way. In general, financial market volatility can be broadly measured. So, when the market becomes difficult to predict, and prices keep on regularly and rapidly changing, the market is volatile.

Volatility can affect option pricing significantly. Many beginning options traders tend to ignore the implications, which can lead to huge investment losses.

## Historical Volatility

Historical or statistical volatility is used to measure the changes in the price of the underlying option, so it's based on actual and real data. Let's refer to it as HV for the rest. HV shows how fast the stock price has moved. The higher HV is, the more the stock price has moved during a specific period. So, when a stock has a high HV, the price is more likely to move, at least theoretically. It's more of a future movement indication and not a real guarantee.

On the other hand, a low HV might indicate the stock price hasn't moved much, but it might be going in one direction steadily.

You can use HV to predict somewhat how much a security's price will change based on how fast it changed in the past, but you can't use it to predict an actual trend.

HV is measured over a certain period, such as a week, month, or year and you can compute for it in various ways.

## Implied Volatility

Another type of volatility that options traders should be aware of is implied volatility or IV. Whereas HV measures a security's past volatility, IV is more of an estimate of its future volatility.

IV is a projection of how fast, and how much the stock price is likely to change in price. Many beginning traders focus on the profitability (difference in strike price and stock price), and the contract expiration when considering an option's price, but IV also plays a significant role.

You can determine an option's IV by considering factors such as the stock and strike prices, length of time before expiration, current interest rate, and HV. Since an option's IV may indicate how much the stock will change in price, the price gets higher when the IV itself increases. Because theoretically, more profit can be gained when there are dramatic movements in the price of the underlying stock. The price of an option can also change significantly even when the stock price remains the same, which is usually caused by its IV.

For example, ABC is about to release a new product, and speculations build-up that the company is about to announce it. The options' IV for stock ABC can be very high since there are expectations of significant movement in the underlying stock price. The announcement might be received well, and the stock price might go up, or the audience will be disappointed with the new product, and stock prices can drop quickly. In this scenario, the stock price might not move since investors will be waiting for the press release before buying or selling stocks. There will then be an increase in extrinsic value for both puts and calls rather than the stock price movement. This is one way that IV can affect option pricing.

If you're betting that a stock's price will dramatically increase once that announcement has been made, you may purchase 'at the money' call options to maximize probable gains for that increase. If ABC announced and was received well, causing the stock prices to shoot up, there would have been significant gains in the call options' intrinsic value. After the press release and the stock price movement, IV will be lower since it's predicted that the stock price won't change very soon. There will then be a substantial fall on the calls' extrinsic value, which would offset most of the profit you gained with the increased intrinsic value.

# CHAPTER 14

## Four Primary Greek Risk Measures

Greeks is a term utilized in the options market to portray the various risk associated dimensions with taking an options position. Each risk variable is a sign of a flawed presumption or relationship of the option with another underlying variable. Traders use Greek qualities, for example, Theta, Delta, and others, to evaluate options risk and oversee option portfolios.

- The 'Greeks' allude to the different components of risk that an options position entails.

- Greeks are utilized by options portfolio and traders' managers to hedge the risk and comprehend how their profit and loss will carry on as prices move.

- The most regular Greeks incorporate the Gamma, Delta, Vega, and Theta, which are the first partial subsidiaries of the options pricing model.

Greeks entail numerous factors. Every last one of these factors/Greeks has a number related to it, and that number enlightens traders concerning how the option moves or the risk related to that option.

The value or number related to Greek changes after some time. Modern options traders may ascertain these qualities every day to survey any progressions that may influence their outlook or position or check if their portfolio should be rebalanced. The following are a few of the primary Greeks traders take a look at.

## Theta

Theta means the rate of change among the time and option price - in some cases known as an option's time decay. Theta shows the sum an option's price would diminish as the time to expiration diminishes, all else equivalent. For instance, assume an investor is long an option with a theta of - 0.50. The option's price would diminish by 50 cents daily, all else being equal.

Theta increments when options are at-the-money, and diminish when options are in-and out-of-the-money. Options closer to lapse likewise have quickening time decay. Long puts and long calls will normally have negative Theta; short puts and calls will have positive Theta. By contrast, an instrument whose worth isn't dissolved by time, for example, a stock, would have zero Theta.

## Vega

Vega implies the rate of change between the underlying assets' implied volatility and an option's value. It demonstrates the sum of an option's value changes, given a 1 percent change in implied volatility. A Vega of 0.10 shows the option's worth is relied upon to change if the implied volatility changes by 1 percent.

Because expanded volatility infers that the underlying instrument is guaranteed to meet extreme values, a rise in volatility will consistently build an option's value. Alternately, a reduction in volatility will adversely influence the value of the option. Vega is at its most extreme for at-the-money options that have longer times until expiration.

Greek-language nerds will call attention to that there is no genuine Greek letter named Vega. Different hypotheses about how this symbol, which takes after the Greek letter nu, found its way into the stock-trading language.

## Delta

Delta means the rate of change between the option's cost and a $1 change in the underlying asset's price. The price sensitivity of the option comparative with the underlying. The Delta of a call option has a range somewhere in the range of zero and one, while the Delta of a put option ranges between zero and a negative one. For instance, assume an investor is long a call option with a delta of 0.50. In this manner, if the underlying stock increments by $1, the option's cost would hypothetically increment by 50 cents.

For options traders, the Delta likewise represents the hedge ratio for making a delta-unbiased position. For instance, if you buy a standard American call option with a 0.40 delta, you should sell 40 shares of stock to be hedged entirely. Net Delta can also be used to get the portfolio's hedge ratio.

Less basic utilization of an option's Delta is the present probability that it will terminate in-the-money. For example, a 0.40 delta call option today has an implied 40% probability of completing in-the-money.

## Gamma

Gamma means the amount of change between an option's Delta and the underlying asset's cost. This is called second-derivative price sensitivity. It shows the sum the Delta would change given a $1 move in the fundamental security. For instance, assume a financial specialist is a long one call option on speculative stock XYZ.

If stock XYZ increments or diminishes by $1, the call option's Delta will increment or decrease by 0.10.

Gamma is utilized to determine how steady an option's Delta is. A higher gamma shows that Delta could change extremely even little movements in the underlying's price. It is higher for options that are at-the-money, and lower for options in-and out-of-the-money and quickens in size as expiration draws near. Gamma values are commonly littler the further away from expiration dates; options with extended expirations are less sensitive to delta changes. As expiration draws near, gamma values are ordinarily more significant, as price changes have more effect on gamma.

## Rho (p)

Rho implies the rate of change between an option's price, and a 1% change in the interest rate. This estimates sensitivity to the interest rate. For instance, expect a call option that has a rho of 0.05, and a cost of $1.25. If the interest rate ascends by 1%, the call option's estimation will increment to $1.30, all else being equal. The inverse is valid for put options. Rho is most prominent for at-the-money options with long times until termination/expiration.

## Minor Greeks

Some different Greeks, which are not discussed often, are epsilon, vomma, lambda, speed, vera, ultima, color, and zomma.

These Greeks are second-or third subordinates of the pricing model and influence things, such as the change in Delta with a change in volatility. They are progressively utilized in options trading strategies as computer programming can rapidly process and record for these complex and sometimes obscure risk factors.

# Conclusion

Options trading is a form of financial speculation that allows investors to buy or sell stock options without owning the underlying stock. This tends to result in much higher returns than investing in stocks directly.

One of options trading's biggest benefits is that it does not require a great deal of initial capital. Even a small sum can be used to buy stock options. However, the cost can quickly add up if large quantities are traded. The monthly premium will need to be paid using the profits generated when the option is exercised.

Options trading is thought to be the more sophisticated form of investing because it allows you to trade for price moves rather than simply for the stock itself. It requires more knowledge and understanding of the market

To use options trading, you must predict how a stock or index will move in the future and what the potential price range is for that move. The more information you learn, the better you'll be able to predict these movements and buy a call or put options accordingly.

You should know the risks involved in options trading. You can reduce some of the risks by trading limit orders, but many traders prefer to trade with both put and call options.

I hope this guide will teach you everything you need to know about options trading, from basics, why people trade options, and how you trade options. It will teach you everything you need to know on this important topic so that you can start making money right now with options trading without having any knowledge at all. You will find out precisely what kinds of investments there are available, and exactly how much your broker will charge for each one so that you can choose the one that is best for your situation.

Options' trading allows you to make money and increase your wealth. There are many different types of options, but most people are familiar with the call option. It is one of the best ways to make money in the stock market. Options are contracts that give you the right, but not the obligation, to buy or sell an asset at a specified price within a specific time frame. Options trading is one of the most popular ways for traders to earn money. However, it's one of the riskiest ways to start making money.

It is very lucrative, but it's also risky because you can lose a lot of money if you don't know what you're doing. Options are a derivative contract that gives the holder the right, but not the obligation, to buy or sell an underlying asset at a set price. Options contracts can be purchased and traded on exchanges. Options trading has become a popular investment strategy for many

www.ingramcontent.com/pod-product-compliance
Lightning Source LLC
Chambersburg PA
CBHW071718210326
41597CB00017B/2519